Life in the Ancient World

Arts and Culture in the Ancient World

Crabtree Publishing Company
www.crabtreebooks.com

Life in the Ancient World

Contributing authors: Paul Challen, Shipa Mehta-Jones,
  Lynn Peppas, Hazel Richardson
Publishing plan research and development:
  Sean Charlebois, Reagan Miller
  Crabtree Publishing Company
Editors: Kathy Middleton, Adrianna Morganelli
Proofreaders: Kathy Middleton, Marissa Furry
Editorial director: Kathy Middleton
Photo research: Katherine Berti, Crystal Sikkens
Designer and prepress technician: Katherine Berti
Print and production coordinator: Katherine Berti

Front cover description:
Top left: From the Han Dynasty in China, this carved, jade
  perfume vessel was used for burning incense.
Top middle: This falcon pendant is inlaid with gems and glass
  and belonged to the pharaoh Tutankhamun of ancient Egypt.
Right: The carvings on the Meenakshi temple in southern India
  depict scenes from the Vedas, the Hindu holy books.
Middle: Built in 161 A.D. the ancient Herodes Atticus theatre is
  located on a hill at the Acropolis, in Greece. It is still used today.
Bottom: This Celtic design is carved into the stone of the Urnes
  Stave Church in western Norway.

Back cover description:
Antique metal box

Title page description:
A Roman tile mosaic in the floor of the Aquileia basilica in Italy

Photographs and reproductions:
Art Resource: Scala: page (bottom); Bildarchiv Preussischer
  Kulturbesitz: page 19;
Corbis: page 8; Stapleton Collection: page 24
iStockPhoto.com: page 11 (top)
Andy Crawford/Dorling Kindersley: page 31
Wikimedia Commons: Orion Hsu: cover (front left); FlickreviewR:
  cover (front center); Haa900: page 3; JovanCormac: page 4; Editor
  at Large: page 6 (left); Vassil; page 6 (right); Bobke: page 7 (top);
  Orion Hsu: page 7 (right); Excavated by Paul-Émile Botta,
  1843–1844 and photographed by Marie-Lan Nguyen: page 9
  (bottom); Astirmays: page 9 (top); Dmharvey: page 9 (middle);
  George Groutas: page 14 (bottom); Captmondo: page 16; John
  Campana: page 17 (top); Didia: page 17 (middle); Marcus Cyron:
  page 17 (bottom); Wolfgang Sauber: pages 21 (bottom left), 29
  (right); Thomas Aleto: page 21 (bottom right); Helvetiker: page
  22; Daderot: page 23 (top and middle right); Luis García: page 23
  (middle left); Paname-IV: page 23 (bottom); Radomil: page 25;
  Jujutacular: page 26 (left); Dennis H.: page 27 (top); Pocopen:
  page 27 (bottom); Zureks: page 28; Dominic Coyne: page 29 (left)
All other images by Shutterstock.com

Illustrations:
William Band: pages 10 (bottom), 30 (right)
Roman Goforth: page 12

Library and Archives Canada Cataloguing in Publication

  Arts and culture in the ancient world.

(Life in the ancient world)
Includes index.
Contributing authors: Paul Challen ... [et al.]
Issued also in electronic formats.
ISBN 978-0-7787-1732-4 (bound).--ISBN 978-0-7787-1739-3 (pbk.)

  1. Art, Ancient--Juvenile literature. 2. Civilization, Ancient--Juvenile literature.
I. Challen, Paul, 1967- II. Series: Life in the ancient world (St. Catharines, Ont.)

N5330.A47 2012   j709.3   C2011-905164-8

Library of Congress Cataloging-in-Publication Data

Arts and culture in the ancient world.
    p. cm. -- (Life in the ancient world)
  Includes index.
  ISBN 978-0-7787-1732-4 (reinforced library binding : alk. paper) -- ISBN 978-0-
7787-1739-3 (pbk. : alk. paper) -- ISBN 978-1-4271-8798-7 (electronic pdf) -- ISBN
978-1-4271-9639-2 (electronic html)
  1. Art, Ancient--Juvenile literature. 2. Civilization, Ancient--Juvenile literature. I.
Crabtree Publishing Company.
  N5330.A69 2012
  930--dc23

                                                  2011029239

Crabtree Publishing Company

www.crabtreebooks.com   1-800-387-7650

Printed in the USA/012014/CG20131129

Published in Canada
Crabtree Publishing
616 Welland Ave.
St. Catharines, Ontario
L2M 5V6

Published in the United States
Crabtree Publishing
PMB 59051
350 Fifth Avenue, 59th Floor
New York, New York 10118

Published in the United Kingdom
Crabtree Publishing
Maritime House
Basin Road North, Hove
BN41 1WR

Published in Australia
Crabtree Publishing
3 Charles Street
Coburg North
VIC, 3058

Contents

Arts and Culture in the Ancient World

Many historians agree that a civilization is a group of people that shares common languages, some form of writing, advanced technology and science, and systems of government and religion. Civilizations also shared similarities in way of life, culture, and art forms, and each was shaped by its stories, artwork, and traditions.

Daily Life and the Arts

Daily life in ancient cultures was influenced by the geography of the civilization's location, the social structure of its society, and the culture's religious practices. Everyone, including women, children, and slaves, had a role to play according to their position.

The social hierarchy, or class system, of an ancient culture determined the kind of work each person did. Artists and writers often held high positions.

As civilizations developed, each culture would create its own art, stories, and traditions. The history of a civilization can be examined through written works that survived, as well as artifacts including pottery, sculpture, jewelry, textiles, and carvings. Examples of art perfected in ancient times include metalwork, glassmaking, printing, theater, and even massage. Through trade, these various art forms were spread among different cultures.

The caste system of the Aryans of the ancient Indus River Valley

Brahmin
scholars
teachers, priests

Kshatriya
kings, warriors
administrators

Vaishya
merchants
agriculturalists
artists

Shudra
artisans
service providers

Maps and Timeline of Ancient Civilizations.

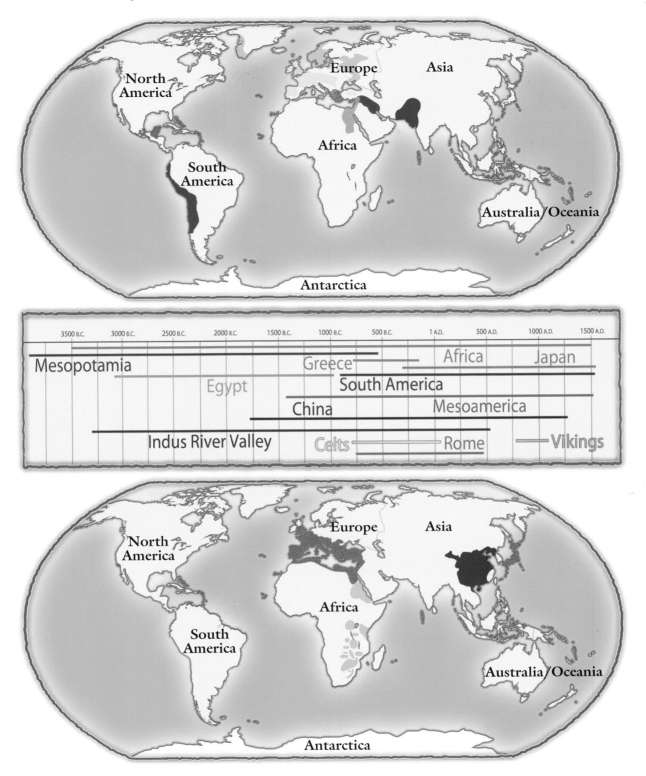

The period described as ancient history is usually defined as the time from first recorded history up to the Early Middle Ages, around 300 A.D. Some of the civilizations in this book begin well after the ancient period but are included because they were dominant early civilizations in their regions. The beginning and ending dates of early civilizations are often subject to debate. For the purposes of this book, the timelines begin with the first significant culture in a civilization and end with the change or disappearance of the civilization. The end was sometimes marked by an event such as invasion by another civilization, or simply by the gradual dispersion of people due to natural phenomena such as famine or earthquakes.

Ancient China

Several dynasties **governed China's enormous land and its large population of farmers, artisans, scholars, merchants, government officials, and slaves. Most ancient Chinese lived lives far different from that of their emperors. However, as China grew from a collection of farming villages into large cities, daily life improved for most and culture flourished.**

1766 B.C.–1271 A.D.

China's people were divided into groups, called social classes, based on birth, wealth, and the kind of work they did. These social classes were the basis of Chinese society. Everything from where people lived to what they ate and wore depended on their social class.

Social Classes

At the top of ancient Chinese society were the ruling dynasties, which included the emperor, his wives and **concubines**, and their immediate families. Members of a dynasty were believed to have been chosen by the spirits of heaven and Earth to rule, and were treated like gods by the people. A large group of royal officials, or bureaucrats, ran the government on a day-to-day basis. Most work, such as farming, building houses, and maintaining roads and canals, was done by farmers.

Regional Cooking

In northern China, boiled noodles, soybeans, and baked breads were common foods. In the south, where farmers planted large rice fields, boiled rice was the main dish, and fresh fruit and seafood were common. In the western mountains, people flavored their food with hot peppers and other spices. Wealthier Chinese often ate meats such as pork, lamb, duck, and pigeon, and for special feasts, snakes, dogs, or bear claws. Most Chinese ate two meals a day. The first meal was at mid-morning and the other came before nightfall. The most important item in the Chinese kitchen was the stove, which burned wood to heat the food.

The Four Arts

Every educated person in ancient China was expected to practice the four arts of music, calligraphy, chess, and brush painting. The ancient Chinese love of the arts spread to include works created by professional artists, musicians, and **scribes** employed by the emperor.

Dress Codes

The clothing, hats, and jewelry worn by a Chinese person showed what position that person held in society. Wealthy people usually wore expensive silk, while peasants wore long shirt-like clothing made of hemp, a fabric woven from plant fiber. Men almost always wore hats when they went out in public.

This pottery figure dates back to the Tang dynasty. It shows the types of clothing wealthy government officials wore.

Noblewomen usually wore their long hair in topknots.

Music

Ancient Chinese music, or *qin*, was played at banquets, ceremonies, and in the court of the emperor and other nobles. Musical instruments, such as the Chinese flute, or *xiao*, date back 9,000 years. The Chinese lute, or *pipa*, was sometimes played by noblewomen at court. During solemn occasions, such as funerals, musicians played bells.

pipa

Calligraphy

Calligraphy, or *shu*, is the Chinese art of depicting written characters on paper. Poets were often calligraphers, who illustrated their poems using the fancy writing. Calligraphers used brushes made from animal hair tied with silk, and fastened into bamboo tubes. Ink was made by rubbing drops of water on a solid inkstone, formed from burned pine soot and gum. It took many years to learn the art of calligraphy.

Brush Painting

The Chinese art of brush painting, or *hua*, dates back at least 6,000 years. Painting was originally done to decorate pottery or bronze statues. After Buddhism arrived in China, painting took on a religious role. Painted religious murals were found in carved grottoes, or caves, as well as in Buddhist temples. By 300 A.D., artists began painting beautiful landscape paintings that were not realistic, but expressed the artists' emotions using soft colors. By the time of the Song Dynasty (960 to 1280 A.D.), people and stories from everyday life had become popular subjects for paintings.

Chinese Chess

Chinese chess was called *qi*. It is based on a game from India called Chaturanga, which may have been brought to China by **Buddhist** missionaries. The game board is set up to represent two enemy countries that are separated by a river. Players move pieces along the lines on the board in an attempt to capture their opponent's king.

Artisans

Many artisans in ancient China created works of art from bronze, jade, and clay. Bronze was made by combining copper and tin. Metalworkers poured molten, or hot liquid, bronze into ceramic molds. When the bronze cooled, the mold was broken to reveal works of art, such as statues, vases, and drinking vessels. The Chinese also used a form of baked clay called terracotta to fashion sculptures and figures.

This perfume censor was carved from white jade stone using an extremely difficult skill known as hollow-out carving.

Kung Fu

Another art that came to China after Buddhism arrived is the martial, or military, art known as kung fu. Kung fu is based on the idea that physical health consists of both inner and outer strength. While physical exercises kept the outer body strong, breathing exercises were meant to help give fuel to the body's inner organs.

By the 1200s, kung fu had spread across Asia. As Chinese kung fu spread, it developed into karate in Japan, and taekwondo in Korea.

Ancient Mesopotamia

Daily life for most people in ancient Mesopotamia was based around agriculture and trade. As trade increased, villages grew into cities, and artisans began to flourish. Mesopotamian potters, carvers, musicians, and metalworkers created objects of beauty to honor important gods, leaders, and historical events.

3900 B.C.–539 B.C.

The wealthiest people in ancient Mesopotamia were government officials, professional soldiers, priests, owners of large parcels of land, and rich traders. Free citizens worked as merchants, farmers, and laborers. Free workers, or clients, were less wealthy and usually rented farmland from free citizens. Most slaves in Mesopotamian society were prisoners of war or citizens who broke the law.

Family Life

A Mesopotamian family was made up of a married couple and their children. Relatives lived together or close to each other. Marriages were arranged by the fathers of the bride and groom. Most men had one wife, but they had the right to marry a second wife if the first was unable to have children.

Homes

Free citizens lived in simple, one-story homes made from sun-dried mud and straw bricks. A room with a drainage hole in the floor served as a bathroom. Each home also had a kitchen with a fireplace and cooking utensils, a shrine for worship, and a reception room where guests could stay overnight. Ladders led to the roof, where people slept on hot summer nights. Several rooms surrounded an open courtyard that let light into rooms.

Homes in the marshlands of southern Mesopotamia were made from bundles of reeds tied together, much like some are today.

Women in Mesopotamia

From childhood, girls were taught to be wives, mothers, and housekeepers, but some also became priestesses, poets, or even tavern-keepers. Women spun and wove cloth, ground grain, cooked, and made beverages, especially beer. Upon her husband's death, a woman fell under the protection of her husband's father or brother, or her grown son. Property was usually passed from father to son, but women could **inherit** land and household furnishings.

Hijab

Women often wore veils, or headscarves, and loose clothing in Assyria. The veil distinguished respectable married women from slaves and unrespectable women, who were not allowed to wear the veil and could be punished by law for doing so. Today, many women in Iraq continue to wear the veils in public, in a custom called *hijab*.

Clothing Through the Ages

The early farmers of Mesopotamia wore clothes made of sheep or goat skins. Men from Sumer, the southern region of Mesopotamia, often wore sheepskin skirts and short capes over their shoulders. Sumerian women wound strips of woven cloth around their bodies and draped the loose end over their shoulder. Babylonian clothing for men and women consisted of full-length, short-sleeved **tunics** and fringed shawls made from brightly dyed and embroidered wool. The Assyrians wore clothing similar to the Babylonians, but added jewelry, such as heavy gold earrings, bracelets, and necklaces. Most Mesopotamians wore leather-soled sandals with heel guards to protect their feet. Until the time of the Assyrians, even soldiers wore sandals into battle. The Assyrians introduced knee-high leather boots with soles that offered protection on rough terrain.

Food

Bread and porridge made from locally grown grains were the main foods in Mesopotamia. Barley, the most common grain, grew well in the south. Other crops included cucumbers, onions, chickpeas, lentils, beans, and lettuce. Dates were one of the most important foods in southern Mesopotamia. Dates could be eaten fresh, dried and preserved, or pressed into a syrup used to sweeten food and drinks. In the north, where it was too cold for date palms to grow, honey was used as a sweetener. Animals were raised and hunted for food. Goats and cows provided milk. People caught fish in rivers, streams, and swamps. Meat was boiled, roasted, or grilled. Most cooking was done in a closed, domed oven or in hot ashes.

Pottery

The earliest Mesopotamian art form was pottery. Pottery was made by layering coils or slabs of clay to form bowls and jars. After about 3500 B.C., the pottery wheel was introduced. The pottery wheel was a surface that revolved as potters worked, allowing the creation of pots with thin, even sides and fancy shapes that were symmetrical. Clay was found all over Mesopotamia. Once shaped, clay vessels were usually baked in an open fire or a kiln.

Metalwork

As cities grew and people became wealthy, demand for precious objects increased. Craftspeople began making jewelry for royalty and the upper classes. As early as 6000 B.C., Mesopotamians made objects out of hammered copper. By 4000 B.C., silver and gold came into use, and bronze in about 2500 B.C. By 1000 B.C., iron was being used to make tools and weapons. Early Mesopotamian statues of gods were made from gold, silver, and bronze. Cups, vases, harps, and lyres were also made of metal. Craftspeople spun gold and silver threads to use in handiwork. It was also common to beat metal into thin sheets and form it into shapes or stamp it with patterns.

The lost wax method was used to cast metal to create several identical objects. It involved carving a model in wax and covering the wax with wet clay, leaving a small hole in the clay cover. The clay-covered model was put in an oven. The clay hardened and the wax melted, draining out the hole. The hole was then filled, and the clay became a cast into which molten, or hot liquid, bronze or glass was poured.

Music of Mesopotamia

Mesopotamians invented some of the earliest known musical instruments, including the harp and the lyre. Music was composed and played to entertain royalty during feasts and gatherings. Hymns were written to praise gods and goddesses, and music often accompanied religious poems and songs. The oldest form of sheet music was carved into clay tablets. Drums and tambourines were also a part of Mesopotamian music.

The Art of Carving

Around 3000 B.C., Sumerians began to carve statues out of stone and use shells as inlay. They also carved decorative patterns on pottery and buildings. The most dramatic carvings found in Mesopotamia are the **reliefs** and statues that decorate palaces and temples. These carvings tell the story of battles or the power of kings.

Sculptures of human-headed, eagle-winged bulls or lions often stood guard at entrances to Assyrian palaces and temples. The crowned head represented supernatural power, the body stood for strength, and the wings for flight and speed.

Ancient Indus River Valley

Two of the world's greatest ancient civilizations—the Harappans and the Aryans—began in the Indus River Valley, in what is now Pakistan. The Harappans were skilled artists and musicians, as well as accomplished stone carvers who erected beautiful temples. Their exciting myths and founding stories are some of the greatest tales ever written. The nomadic **Aryans** intermixed with the Harappans. Their holy books, called the Vedas, are a historical record of their lives.

3300 B.C.–550 A.D.

Tribal Life

The Aryans lived in *ganas*, which means "collections." A *gana* was made up of several families. Each *gana* had its own territory, ruled by a warrior chief called a *raja*, or king. Most *gana* houses were small and built of wood and straw and had only one room, where all family members lived. Historians believe that the families of rulers and nobles lived in larger homes.

Fireside Tales

Aryan homes had a central hearth, called the *yagna*. Family members gathered around the *yagna* to eat and share news of the day. Food was cooked over the fire using roasting spits and bronze cauldrons. The Aryans ate fruit, vegetables, wheat, barley, rice, beef, goat, and mutton, or sheep. They also made butter from cow milk and drank cow and goat milk. The fire tender of the household had the important task of keeping the *yagna's* fire going. Fire was considered a gift from Agni, the fire god.

The Caste System

The Aryans in the Indus Valley belonged to castes, or social levels. People were born into castes and could not move up or down. Aryan priests were *brahmans*, the highest social level. Warriors and rulers were *kshatriyas*. Farmers were members of the *vaisyas* caste, and servants and laborers were *sudras*. The Aryans called the indigenous people of the Indus Valley *dasas*, or the untouchables. *Dasas* were considered the lowest level in society. All caste members had to eat food prepared by members of their own caste, work in caste-specific jobs, and marry within their caste. Those who married outside their caste could be killed.

Women and Children

Until about 500 B.C., Aryan women were allowed to own property. Some were even famous warriors. Over time, the *brahmans* became powerful and developed new ideas, including the idea that women should be strictly controlled. A woman was not allowed to own property and had a husband chosen for her by her parents. Women were taught to obey male members of their family.

Most Aryan children began working at a young age. Farmers' sons herded animals, while daughters did housework and fetched water. Boys of the *brahman* caste went to school to learn the **sacred** Vedas from *gurus*. Boys from wealthy families were taught mathematics and astronomy, but girls had no formal education.

An Aryan man placed a spot of his blood on his bride's forehead as a sign that she belonged to him.

Yards of Tradition

The traditional Indian dress for women was a *sari*. The *sari* is a long piece of silk or cotton cloth draped around the body and sometimes the head. Many peasant men in India wore a *dhoti*, a piece of cloth wrapped around the waist and between the legs. Both are still worn today.

Magnificent Temples

The greatest artworks of ancient Indian civilization are its temples. By 400 B.C., Indians were skilled stoneworkers, having learned from the ancient Greeks, with whom they traded. From 320 A.D. to 540 A.D., beautiful stone temples with magnificent carvings were built all over northern India.

Harappan Art

Music, beauty, and art were important to the Harappans. They invented stringed musical instruments that looked like harps, and filled their towns and cities with beautiful statues, carved pottery, and furniture inlaid with precious stones.

Ancient Indian Festivals

Ancient Indians had more festivals and holy days than any other civilization. People fasted, bathed, chanted, drank, and offered gifts to *brahmans*. One festival celebrated the birthday of Ganesh, the elephant-headed god of luck, believed to have been born while his mother, the love goddess, Parvati, was having a bath. Worshipers at Ganesh festivals broke open coconuts in front of clay figures of Ganesh to show they destroyed their pride.

Movie Heroes

Today, thousands of movies are made each year in India. Many Indian movies recreate ancient Indian myths and legends, including hymns from the Vedas. The movies keep history alive and teach moviegoers about the culture of ancient India. Most Indian movies are made in modern Mumbai, formerly known as Bombay, India's Hollywood or Bollywood. The movies almost always feature singing and dancing adapted from ancient, or classical Indian dance, and stories of ancient battles.

(above) The sari is a long piece of silk or cotton cloth draped around the body, and sometimes the head.

(above) Festivals honoring Ganesh's birth are still celebrated in modern India.

(right) This statue of a dancing girl is the most famous piece of Harappan art. Music and dancing were important parts of Harappan life.

Ancient Greece

800 B.C.–146 B.C.

Ancient Greek society depended on people doing different tasks. The wealthy lived a life of leisure, often serving in politics or debating philosophy. Many people were farmers, while others were teachers, merchants, sailors, metalworkers, and marble workers. Most hard labor was done by slaves.

Home Greek Home

Within a city's walls, homes were crowded close together. The homes were one story, with painted mud-brick walls set on stone foundations. Flat roofs provided a place where families gathered in the cool of the evening. Windows were high and had wooden shutters to give privacy from the bustle in the streets. Wealthy Greeks lived in two-story homes that looked inward over an open courtyard.

No central heating was needed in Greece's warm climate. Some rooms had beautiful **mosaic** floors and **frescoed** walls, where scenes of gods and everyday life were painted onto the wet plaster. Carved chests, tables, couches, and three-legged chairs provided comfort, and carpets and curtains added more color. Homes did not have a private bath or well. People got water at the public fountain at the agora, or marketplace.

Every home had a hearth for cooking and an altar where sacrifices were made to the gods.

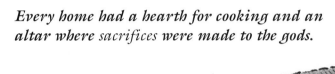

Women lived in a separate part of the house called the gynaeceum.

Servants prepared meals in the kitchen.

Banquets were held in the dining room, or andron.

Women's Quiet Lives

A woman's role in ancient Greek society depended on whether she was married and in which **city-state** she lived. A married woman in Athens stayed home, in separate quarters, away from the windows. She could go out in public for a special occasion, such as a funeral, religious festival, or family visit, as long as she was accompanied by a member of her household. It was her job to raise children, spin wool and **flax**, and weave it into bedding and clothes. She had to manage servants or slaves and care for them when they were ill. Athenian women could not vote, own land, or participate in business. In the city-state of Sparta, women could own property and manage it. Women were not formally educated, but some women could read and write. Often, a girl left home at about age fifteen for married life with a much older man who was chosen by her father.

Slaves and Metics

In Athens, slaves did the backbreaking work. Slaves were abandoned infants, prisoners of war, criminals, or individuals bought at market from the slave traders. Slaves could not raise their own children, but they were not taxed or forced into military service. A freedman was a slave who earned his freedom by buying it from his master. Other manual laborers were metics. Metics were foreigners, or people from other places. Sometimes metics became wealthy saving the money they earned. Metics could not vote, marry an Athenian, or own property. Metics still had to pay taxes and do military service.

What's On the Menu?

Poorer families in ancient Greece ate barley cakes, called *maza*, and enjoyed meat only during festivals. When times were good, they added goat's cheese, olives, salted fish, **legumes**, and vegetables to the menu. The wealthy ate lamb, goat, pig, or dog every day. They drank wine, and had bread baked from grains such as wheat or barley. Flatbreads, such as pita, were used as an edible **utensil** to pick up food cooked in sauces. The seas provided fish and seafood. Poorer people ate salted and dried fish, while the wealthy ate shark meat, eel, and octopus.

Clothing

Clothing in ancient Greece consisted of a loose-fitting tunic. A cloak was worn in cooler weather and on special occasions. In times of peace, fashions of the wealthy were showy and colorful. During war, fancy dress was not worn. Around 550 B.C., the *chiton* became popular. The chiton was a linen garment imported from the east that men and women wore. Wealthy Greeks wore leather sandals, although many people went barefoot in the summer. Wealthy men and women wore their hair long. Women wore elaborate hairstyles or wigs. Men fastened their hair up with a gold brooch. Greek men grew beards and women used makeup made from plants to redden their cheeks and whiten their skin.

Here Comes the Bride

Marriage in ancient Greece was a business deal between the parents of the bride and groom. A girl's father offered the groom a dowry, which consisted of money, clothing, jewelry, animals, or slaves. If he accepted, the wedding was arranged. Before the wedding, a bride had a ceremonial bath and put on bright clothes and a veil. The wedding began with an all-day feast at the bride's home. Then the groom led the bride to his family's house, with guests holding torches to light the darkened streets and musicians playing flutes and lyres. The newlyweds ate wedding cake made from sesame seeds and honey. The act of sharing food in her husband's home sealed the marriage bond.

chiton

sandals

13

Greek Arts and Culture

Greek arts and culture reached their height in Athens from 500 B.C. to 400 B.C. The ancient Greeks left an amazing legacy to the entire world of art and architecture, poetry and drama, and philosophy and science. They believed their pottery, sculpture, and architecture needed to honor the gods. Poetry and plays told stories of exciting or tragic events that were influenced by the gods.

Pottery

The best pottery in ancient Greece came from Athens. Potters used a special local clay to make vases of many shapes and sizes in a reddish-brown color. These vases were used to carry, store, and mix water, wine, and olive oil. Vases were also traded widely around the Greek world. Before 530 B.C., vases were decorated with black figures on a red background. Later, red figures on a black background became popular.

Sculpture

Sculpture was an important part of the ancient Greek world. Early Greek sculptors admired and copied the statues of the ancient Egyptians, which they saw on trading voyages. The Greeks used a stone called white marble to create life-size statues known as *kourai* if they are male or *korai* if they are female. These statues were used to mark graves and to serve as memorials outside of temples. Later sculptors made more detailed sculptures of gods, statesmen, military heroes, athletes, and wealthy citizens. These statues were made of marble and were painted with vivid colors. Some statues were made of bronze. Statues often decorated public buildings and the homes of ordinary citizens.

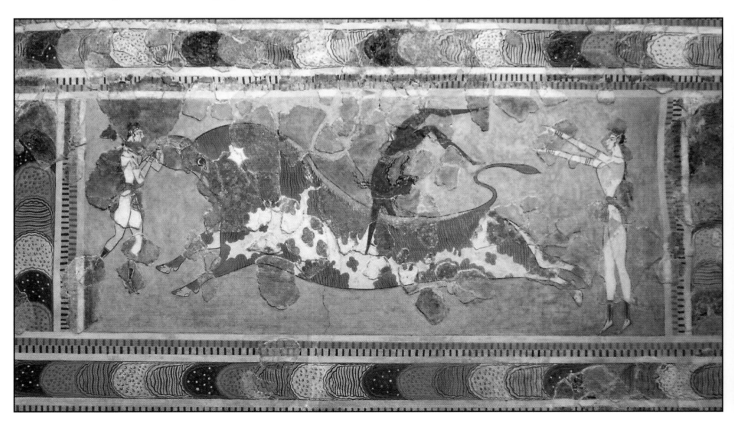

Frescoes are made by applying colorful paint to wet plaster so that the color becomes fixed as the plaster dries. On the island of Crete, the Minoans decorated palaces and wealthy homes with frescoes.

Theater

The ancient Greeks enjoyed both tragic and comic drama as far back as 500 B.C. Most cities had an open-air theater, or amphitheater, where plays were performed during the day. Some plays were put on as part of religious festivals honoring Dionysus, the god of wine and drama. Some festivals were competitions in which playwrights won a prize for the best play. At the beginning of a play, a chorus of actors stood in a circular area called the orchestra and sang or recited lines to the audience, describing what was taking place on stage. The chorus wore frowning, angry, smiling, or surprised masks to show their mood. Then the actors spoke to the chorus. Only three men performed on stage but they played more than one part, including the female roles.

Epic Poetry

Stories about heroes and their deeds were told by ancient Greek poets in long poems called epics. Epic poems were oral at first and written down many years later. The most famous Greek epics, the *Iliad* and the *Odyssey*, were composed by a blind poet named Homer around 700 B.C. The *Iliad* describes the long war between the Greeks and the people of Troy that began when a Trojan prince kidnapped the beautiful Greek queen, Helen. To get her back, the Greeks sent a large army, which included the Greek hero Achilles. After ten years of fighting, the Greeks rescued Helen and burned Troy to the ground. The *Odyssey* tells the story of Odysseus, a hero who spent ten years traveling home after the Trojan War. Along the way, Odysseus faced many terrible challenges, including a fight with a one-eyed creature called the Cyclops.

Great Playwrights

The ancient Greeks wrote many plays, some of which are still performed all around the world. The playwrights Aeschylus, Sophocles, and Euripides wrote tragedies. In tragedies, the main character faced challenges. A tragedy's ending was unhappy and the main character often died or was punished by the gods. Aristophanes wrote comedies. A comedy often poked fun at politics and people. It usually had a happy ending.

Alexander the Great

By 338 B.C., King Philip of Macedon had conquered Athens, Sparta, and most other Greek city-states. His son, known as Alexander the Great, expanded Philip's kingdom to include Egypt, India, and Persia. Alexander thought highly of Greek culture. He settled Greeks in the conquered cities. The Macedonian conquest changed the Greek way of life, but it also preserved and spread Greek culture. This period in history is known as the Hellenistic Age because Alexander spread Greek philosophy, language, art, and science throughout his empire.

Aristotle was a Greek philosopher who wrote about nature, science, math, and politics. He once worked as a tutor to Alexander the Great, who later conquered most of the world.

Sappho's Lyric Legacy

One of the few female poets of ancient Greece was Sappho, who lived sometime between 650 B.C. and 750 B.C. Sappho wrote poetry on the island of Lesbos. Until Sappho's time, poetry was mainly written from the point of view of the gods. Sappho changed this by writing poems about love and loss from her own point of view. Her poetry was written to be accompanied by a musical instrument called the lyre, which is why she is often called a lyric poet.

Ancient Egypt

In ancient Egypt, a small group, including the pharaoh and his nobles, priests, and government officials, were at the top of the social pyramid. Everyday life, however, depended on the millions of slaves, servants, and farmers laboring at the bottom. Throughout the year Egyptians marked harvest and religious events with feasts where musicians and dancers entertained. Egyptian artists recorded scenes from these events on walls or tomb chapels.

Home Sweet Home

Egyptian pharaohs and nobles lived in large homes made of stone, tile, and sun-baked bricks. The huts of farmers and craftsmen were made from mud and straw bricks that were dried in the sun and later painted white. Homes of farmers were only one or two rooms, while pharaohs and nobles had living quarters with shrines, banquet rooms, painted audience halls, broad corridors, balconies, formal gardens and pools, workshops, breweries, and stables.

Clothing

Egypt's hot weather required comfortable clothing. Ancient Egyptians wore clothing made from linen, a strong fabric made from the fibers of flax plants. Women wore long dresses while men often wore a kilt wrapped at the waist. When it was cooler, people wore a thick cloak over these light garments. Nobles wore leather sandals. Farmers and servants either did not wear shoes or wore sandals made from the tough stalks of Nile reed plants. Nobles at court and wealthy citizens wore wigs and fancy headdresses and jewelry of gold and gemstones.

Women in Egypt

Women in ancient Egypt were expected to teach daughters in the home but many also had other jobs. Some women served in the pharaoh's palace as acrobats, dancers, singers, and musicians. Others worked for wealthy families as maids. Women could not hold government positions or inherit the title of pharaoh. Queen Hatshepsut ignored this rule and governed Egypt after the death of her husband Pharaoh Thutmose II. She had to dress like a man in order to keep power.

A Child's Life

Only boys from wealthy or noble families attended school. They learned how to write with ink on papyrus and by carving **hieroglyphs** into pieces of clay. Older boys studied history, geography, science, and mathematics. Other boys learned a trade or craft from their fathers. Girls stayed home with their mothers and learned cooking and other skills they would need to run a household. Girls did not attend school, but girls from wealthy families were taught to read and write, and helped manage the estate. Some even trained at home to become doctors. Children also cared for elderly parents. Upon their parents' death, both sons and daughters inherited land.

Games They Played

Egyptian children played with clay and wooden balls, tops, toy animals, and dolls. The games were made by craftspeople who handed their skills down to their children. Young and old enjoyed board games, especially a game called senet in which two players moved pieces around 30 squares on a wooden board. The winner was the first person to reach the kingdom of the god Osiris.

For wealthy families, fishing expeditions on the Nile were a favorite sport. Wealthy Egyptians also hunted ducks, geese, and cranes in the papyrus reeds along the river. Hunting big game such as hippopotamus or crocodile required longer trips into the wilderness. Nobles also rode into the desert with packs of trained hunting dogs in pursuit of gazelle, antelope, foxes, and lions.

This board game was found in the tomb of an ancient Egyptian pharaoh. It is similar to a popular game called senet.

Party!

Harvest and religious festivals were major events for the ancient Egyptians. The pharaoh and noble families held celebrations where guests dined on fattened cattle, wild fowl, wild antelope, gazelle, and ibex hunted nearby. Cooks prepared fancy meals using vegetables such as beans, lentils, herbs, and spices, along with a variety of fruits and coarse **yeast** bread. Guests drank ale made from barley, and wine made from grapes, dates, figs, and pomegranates. Musicians and acrobats entertained people as they ate. Women put aromatic cones of fat on their headdresses and as it slowly melted, it bathed their wigs with sweet-smelling fragrance.

Skilled metalworkers made fine jewelry for wealthy Egyptians. Thin strips of metal were welded into designs. Gold, turquoise, and carnelian were used to decorate jewelry.

Design and Crafts

Objects of daily life, including sandals, rings, clothing, and drinking pots were made by leatherworkers, jewelers, cabinetmakers, weavers, and potters. Some of their work survives today. Gold and gems such as turquoise, carnelian, and amethyst were plentiful in ancient Egypt. Jewelers used them to decorate necklaces, bracelets and anklets. Wooden beds, carrying chairs, chariots and cosmetics boxes inlaid with ivory have been found in Egyptian tombs. The tomb of Pharaoh Tutenkhamen contained an alabaster vase to hold costly oils, royal daggers inlaid with bronze, and feathered fans.

(Above) women play lutes and a flute to entertain guests at a party. Other common Egyptian instruments included lyres, cymbals, drums, and harps.

Religious Art

The Valley of the Kings is an area in central Egypt where many of the pharaohs of the New Kingdom (1600 B.C. to 1070 B.C.) were buried in tombs. Inside the tombs were long corridors and secret rooms with walls covered in bright paintings. In the paintings, the pharaoh was depicted as a god. In some tombs, the artwork showed hunting scenes, farmers working the fields, dancing, games, animals, foreign visitors, and court ceremonies.

Protecting Egyptian Treasures

European explorers began to dig up Egyptian artifacts in the 1800s. Egyptologists, or archaeologists who specialize in Egypt, found important Egyptian artifacts and gave them to museums around the world. Today, Egypt does not allow archaeologists to take objects out of the country. Sometimes, grave robbers and smugglers steal the artifacts and offer them for sale outside the country. Egypt has asked that these items be returned. It has also set up a special committee to look into stolen antiquities, or ancient treasures. Several important artifacts have been returned, including the mummy of Ramses I, which was looted from the Valley of the Kings in 1871. It is against the law to buy an Egyptian artifact in Egypt today.

Ancient Africa

Life for many ancient Africans was based on farming, fishing, herding, hunting, and later, trading. Many families lived together in circular groups of houses, called compounds. Ancient African art, jewelry, carvings, and paintings reflected the people's relationship to the land and animals, as well as their beliefs in gods who controlled the natural world. Music, dance, and storytelling were also an important part of daily life.

Farming and Herding

Many ancient African cultures were farming or **pastoral** societies. Cattle were herded as domestic livestock in the central Saharan highlands as far back as 5000 B.C. Both nomadic and semi-nomadic cattle herders lived on the grasslands throughout Africa. Some built permanent settlements of mud houses with nearby cattle enclosures. In farming cultures, each person had a role in making sure that there was enough food to eat. Men fished, farmed, or herded animals, moving them around the countryside to take advantage of green pastures. Women were farmers who also looked after their children, worked in the fields, and prepared food. Many ancient African societies kept slaves who were often war captives from other cultures. Slaves usually had no choice in what work they did but some slaves achieved positions of power. Slaves were traded among other cultures and some even served as soldiers in ancient armies.

The Nubians

Most ancient Nubians lived in the countryside in round houses. These houses were built from wood posts covered with mud, with cone-shaped roofs made with grass. Nubian men wore short skirts or loincloths made from cheetah or gazelle skins. Women wore leather or linen skirts, and kept their upper bodies uncovered. Most people ate bread or a porridge made from grains they farmed, such as barley. Nobles could afford to eat roasted fish, beef, and wild foods, such as antelope and gazelle. They also ate vegetables and fruit, including lentils, chickpeas, dates, and figs.

The Aksumites

Most houses in ancient Aksum were built by covering stone or wood with mud. In wealthy homes, clay pipes carried warm air from an oven below the floor to heat the rooms. Peasants and slaves wore simple leather clothing, while the wealthy wore cotton or sometimes silk cloth that was draped around the body. A common meal for Aksumites was a spicy stew made from beef, lentils, peas, and hot pepper. They also ate pancakes made from a cereal grain called teff.

People from many ancient African cultures lived in thatched-roof houses made from mud, and often, cow dung. The houses were cool in summer and warm in winter.

Ancient Ghana

Peasant houses in ancient Ghana were made of mud bricks or wood and had only one room. In the cities, houses were larger and built of mud bricks. Ancient books describe the home of Ghana's king as surrounded by a large enclosure, like a city wall. The king and his government ministers wore clothing of fine cotton while most ancient Ghanians wore rough-hewn cotton garments. The king also wore his hair plaited with gold. Traders, made wealthy by Ghana's gold trade, wore clothing made from linen cloth imported from Egypt and Greece. The main crops grown in the area included millet, cotton, and sorghum, a plant similar to corn.

Ancient Mali

In ancient Mali, peasants lived in villages made up of small circular compounds, which were each surrounded by a wall. Members of related families lived within each compound. Men herded goats and sheep and grew millet and rice. Women made meals of boiled rice, bread made from millet, and fish or lamb stew. They also cooked, cleaned, cared for the children, and worked in the fields.

Nubian Art

The Nubians were the first civilization in the world to develop a large-scale iron **smelting** industry for producing metal goods, and much of their greatest artwork was made of iron. Nubian artisans also made priceless golden treasures, including the masks found in Egyptian pyramids and tombs.

Benin Bronze Art

The kingdom of Benin is best known for the large, lifelike brass and bronze heads made in honor of the kings. The heads, displayed in the palace, were usually images of the king, but sometimes were of members of the king's family. Bronze snakes decorated the royal palace in Benin and were a symbol of Osun, the god of nature. Benin artisans also made brass and bronze plaques for the palace that showed the history of Benin. The people of Benin considered the leopard the king of beasts and used it as a symbol of royal power in their art. Many bronze objects made for the king were of this wild cat.

Ancient Zimbabwe Carvings

Animal imagery was common in the art of ancient Zimbabwe. Household items were decorated with simple carvings of many types of animals. The most famous pieces of art found in the city of Great Zimbabwe are bird sculptures carved from soapstone.

Jewelry

Ancient Africans made most of their jewelry from gold. Nubians wore gold neck rings, arm bracelets, earplugs, and headbands. Attendants to the king of Ghana were described as having their hair braided with gold, while the king wore a golden cap, necklace, and bracelet.

This Nubian gold ring shows the lion-headed god of royal power, Apedemak.

Music and Dance

Music was important to many aspects of ancient African life. It provided entertainment and accompanied games, contests, stories, and religious ceremonies. At festivals and special occasions, musicians played bone flutes and other instruments, while the other villagers played along with wooden drums and shakers, clapped their hands, and stomped their feet or danced. Royal courts kept their own musicians. Their instruments, including ivory trumpets, harps, and drums carved with the images of animals and gods, were seen as a sign of prestige.

African Folklore

Traditional beliefs and myths, many about birds, were passed down from generation to generation in ancient Africa through storytelling. Several birds, including hawks and eagles, were believed to be messengers of the gods. Many tales told of migrating birds bringing **fertility** with them. In others, birds were reincarnated, or reborn, humans. Taking eggs from a bird's nest was thought to bring bad luck.

Women of Ancient Africa

Women's roles within the family and society differed throughout ancient Africa. In most cultures, women were the primary caregivers for children and the elderly. Women also kept their families fed by working in the fields, milking cows, harvesting crops, winnowing grain, and also by preparing meals. Other women worked as potters, traders, weavers, and dyers.

Life for most women was very difficult. Many women were slaves. Some women of wealth, royalty, and privilege were educated. In some cultures, women were priestesses who cared for shrines and temples, performed rituals to communicate with the gods, and healed people using herbs. In ancient Egypt and Aksum, many women owned property. Nubian and Egyptian women could become rulers. Women in some areas of Africa could even become chiefs.

Ancient Mesoamerica

1400 B.C.–1521 A.D.

In ancient Mesoamerica, the way people lived depended on their position and role in society. The ruling elite formed a very small part of Mesoamerican civilization, and daily life depended on ordinary people working the farms, building temples, and fighting wars. Mesoamericans created art, sculpture, pottery, and architecture that reflected their beliefs, as well as their daily lives. Most of the ancient art and architecture has been destroyed by time, the climate, or by human hands.

Farmers

Most Mesoamericans were farmers. Farmers' lives revolved around maize, or corn. If maize grew, the people could eat. If maize did not grow, the people would starve. Farmers were required to grow more maize than they could use themselves. The extra maize was used to pay tribute to the ruler of their city-state. The ruler would advise farmers when to plant crops and he arranged religious rituals and sacrifices to gain the favor of the gods, so crops would be plentiful. When they were not working the land, farmers worked on construction in the city. Farmers were also required to fight in wars.

Most Mesoamericans lived in one-room homes with floors made of clay and covered with river sand. Family members slept on mats on the floor. Walls were made from canes or reeds, held up between wood posts. The spaces in between were filled with mud and then **white-washed**. Roofs were **thatched**, or covered with palm tree leaves. Kings and emperors lived in stone palaces and temple-pyramids that still exist in places such as Tikal in Guatemala. Priests and nobles lived in homes made of adobe, or sun-dried clay, bricks.

thatched roof

cane or reeds

A simple Maya home was only one room.

A Woman's Place

Women were not accepted as the equal of men in Mesoamerica. Most women took care of the household, made meals and clothing, and cared for children. In a few royal families, a woman filled the role of ruler when the king was unable. Some royal and noble women also took part in ritual sacrifices of humans, and worked as healers, midwives, and priestesses.

Mesoamericans usually married around the age of 20. The wedding ceremony took place at night and the bride was delivered to the groom on the back of an elderly woman. Instead of exchanging rings and kisses, the bride and groom tied their blouse and cloak together. Royal families of different city-states often married to strengthen ties between their communities.

Clothing

Mesoamerican men wore loincloths, which were strips of cloth that wrapped around their waists and covered them to the tops of their thighs, and sleeveless capes. Women wore long cotton skirts with blouses. The use of color and feathers separated the wealthy nobles from the poorer people. Wealthy Mesoamericans could afford brighter designs on fine cotton. Farmers wore plain, white maguey cloth that was not as soft or ornate as cotton. Only nobles and kings wore elaborate headdresses, often made with the brilliant green tail feathers of the sacred quetzal bird.

(above) Mayan Jaina King with elaborate headdres

Ancient Arts

Around 300 A.D., Mesoamericans began creating large, rectangular stone panels called stelae. The stone panels outside temple-pyramids were carved to show rulers or high priests. Some carvings showed important historical events, such as great battles. Important women were sometimes shown in the carvings, elaborately dressed with large headdresses and jewelry. Accounts of the life and death of the person on the panel were written along the sides.

Mesoamericans were skilled musicians. The Maya made instruments out of turtle shells and gourds. Drums were also made by hollowing out logs, or from clay pots covered in animal skins. Small pottery figurines shaped like people, or sometimes half-animal, half-human creatures, were used as whistles.

Ancient Mesoamericans pierced and tattooed their bodies to make themselves beautiful. They also filed their teeth to a point. The Maya changed the shape of their babies' skulls to resemble the maize god's elongated head, which they considered beautiful. They did this by tying two boards to the front and back of infants' heads for several days after birth. The Maya also pierced ears with large earrings. They made tattoo-like scars on their bodies with paint made from crushed flowers and insects.

Jewelry was crafted using precious stones such as jadeite, diopside, or serpentine. Jade was often fashioned into masks or figurines for royal burials, containers for rituals, and jewelry for the wealthy.

These Mayan hieroglyphs are carved onto a stela, or stone pillar.

Slaves

Mesoamerican slaves were mainly captured warriors. In Aztec society, slaves were the lowest class of people but they did have some rights. Aztec slaves could save money and buy houses or land. Slaves could marry free Aztecs, and children born of these marriages were recognized as free people. If an Aztec slave escaped and ran fast enough to the ruler's palace without being caught by his owner, the slave could win his freedom.

On the Menu

Maize was an important food for Mesoamericans. Maize kernels were removed from the cob and soaked overnight to soften. Often, a rock called limestone was added to the water to make the kernels more tender. The kernels were then ground with stones into meal and formed into a loaf. The loaf was cooked on top of a clay, three-pronged oven, similar to a barbecue.

The Game of Champions

Throughout Mesoamerica, a ball game associated with both religion and war was played. The object of the game was to get a rubber ball through a stone ring on the side of the court wall. A player wore paddles at the sides of his waist which he used to hit the ball. Both Maya and Aztec art depicts losing teams being sacrificed. Rulers played the ball game against their captives to decide who would live and who would die. The rulers always won. Losers had their heads cut off at the end of the game.

A statue shows a ball player wearing padding for protection.

Ancient South America

The ancient civilizations that developed in the Andes mountains of South America did not have systems of writing, so historians study artwork and other artifacts to learn what their lives were like. Ruled by high priests or kings, most people were farmers or artisans who supported the rulers and their families by giving them food and items they produced. Pottery, textiles, and metalwork showed scenes from everyday life such as hunting, battles, worship, and the lives of rulers.

900 B.C.–1572 A.D.

Food and Shelter

Coastal homes were built of wooden posts that were covered in mud. The roofs were flat and thatched with grass. Mountain homes were made of stone blocks, with peaked thatched roofs to let the rain run off. The rulers' palaces were located in city centers and were made of stone. Parts of their outer walls were covered with gold.

Ancient Andeans ate their main meal in the evening. The meal was usually a stew made of potatoes, beans, and other vegetables, such as maize, or corn, peppers, squash, and chilies. On festival days and other special occasions, people roasted maize cobs and guinea pigs. The most common drink for both children and adults was *chicha*, a mild beer made from **fermented** maize.

Women and Children

Inca women tended to the crops in the fields, and took care of the animals. Mothers strapped their babies onto their backs so they could work in the fields and look after their children at the same time. Children were expected to work from an early age. They helped their parents by doing tasks, such as keeping animals away from the crops and taking care of the llamas.

Making Cloth

On the coast, where it was warmer, people grew cotton and wove it into fabric to make clothing. In the mountains, cloth was woven from llama wool. Nobles wore clothing made from the fine wool of the alpaca or vicuna, animals similar to llamas. Dyes made from plants, and cochineal, a type of insect, were used to color fabric purple and red. **Iron oxide** was used to dye fabric orange. Textiles were woven with **geometric** patterns of lines, animal shapes, and plants. Gold and silver thread was stitched into the clothing worn by the ruling classes.

Styles of Dress

Men wore a wraparound skirt and a simple shirt, or a knee-length tunic, sometimes with a woolen poncho over top to keep warm. Women wore ankle-length dresses and a shawl. Both men and women wore sandals made of llama hide or slippers woven from grass. Nobles decorated themselves with gold and silver necklaces and bracelets. People of all ages and social classes wore caps called *chucus*, woven from llama or alpaca wool. These were often fastened to the head with a woven headband.

Chavín Crafts

The Chavín decorated their pottery with a variety of carefully repeated patterns, including figure eights, circles, and curls. Simple figures of people and animals were also common. The Chavín were expert goldsmiths. They hammered gold into thin sheets, which they shaped into masks and pots. They also wove alpaca wool into beautiful rugs and blankets. Alpaca textiles were valuable and were mostly owned by priests and nobles. The Chavín decorated their textiles with the same patterns as their pottery. They also made a musical instrument by punching small holes into a large seashell. A musician played the instrument by blowing into the shell, like a trumpet, and covering the holes with his or her fingers to create different notes.

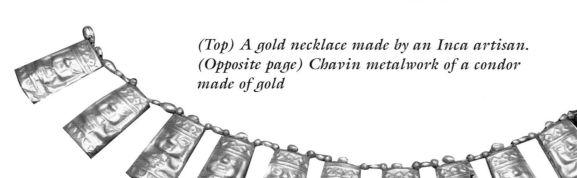

(Top) A gold necklace made by an Inca artisan.
(Opposite page) Chavin metalwork of a condor made of gold

Inca Metalwork

The Incas were the most advanced metalworkers of all the ancient Andean civilizations. Artisans used bronze and copper to make spearheads and tools, such as knives. They made ceremonial masks, dishes and pots, jewelry, and even thread from gold and silver. These precious metals were so plentiful that the Incas covered parts of their palaces and temples with gold. Life-size gold and silver statues of llamas, corn stalks, and female figures stood in the courtyards of the most important temples.

Moche Pottery

The Moche are known for their lifelike three-dimensional portrait vessels, crafted to depict priests and rulers. These vessels, which were placed in the graves of dead rulers, were usually of heads only, but sometimes showed the full body. The Moche also made spout pots, like the Chavín, decorating them with vivid scenes of battles, religious ceremonies, and everyday life. Images of warriors show that the Moche used clubs and shields as weapons.

Nazca Textiles

The Nazca peoples were expert weavers of cotton and llama and alpaca wool. They created fine lace and enormous pieces of textile. The cloth was woven with brightly colored geometric figures of birds, animals, and people. Textiles were used to make head coverings that protected the head and neck from the sun. They were also used as robes for wrapping the dead.

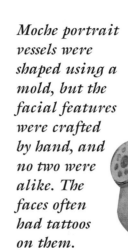

Moche portrait vessels were shaped using a mold, but the facial features were crafted by hand, and no two were alike. The faces often had tattoos on them.

The Nazca decorated their textiles with detailed geometric patterns and images of animals and gods.

23

Ancient Rome

753 B.C.– 476 A.D.

The quality of daily life in ancient Rome depended on the goodwill of the emperor. During Trajan's reign, roads and aqueducts **were built and money was given to the poor. Under emperors Caligula and Caracalla, so many citizens were murdered, both emperors were thought to be insane. The arts were valued in ancient Rome, but Romans generally adopted the ideas of other peoples, especially the Greeks. They created literature and poetry, but were most famous for orations, or speeches.**

The Order of Things

The patricians were the upper class of Roman society, including priests, army officers, and government. The 300 senators who ran the empire came from this class. The equites were businessmen who were not as wealthy as patricians but rich enough to own a ship for overseas trade. Those not involved in overseas trade supervised the building of temples or aqueducts, or owned shops.

The plebeians were farmers, artisans, doctors, fishermen, stonecutters, or shopkeepers. Some plebeians were gladiators who fought wild beasts in the arena, or drove chariots at the circus, an outdoor racetrack. Clients were poor plebeians who received daily handouts from wealthy men. In return, clients greeted their patron each morning and promoted his good name around the town. Hundreds of thousands of people lived in Rome, most of them in crowded slums. A housing shortage, along with crime in the streets and soaring rents, meant that the ordinary person lived a life of misery.

The lowest class in Rome were slaves. Slaves were usually captured in war and had no rights in society. They worked for no pay and little food until they were too sick or old to work and were then abandoned. Those who did construction or dug mines had it the worst.

Family Life

The family was the center of Roman society. The father, or paterfamilias, was like a king. He had control and power over all his children as long as he lived. A father decided how his wife, children, grandchildren, clients, and slaves lived. Roman children were raised to be healthy and strong so they could grow up to farm and fight to defend Rome. Fathers decided if newborn babies would be accepted into the family. Babies who were ill or deformed were often abandoned in a public place. If they survived, they usually became slaves.

Clothing

Men, women, and children, rich and poor, wore wool or linen tunics. Tunics are simple, short-sleeved, ankle-length garments that were slipped on over the head. In cooler weather, a cloak was worn on top. Patricians draped a huge cloth in folds, called a toga, around the body. Senators wore a crimson stripe on their togas from shoulder to hem so they stood out. Gold jewelry was popular for the wealthy. Women often had their ankle-length tunics and cloaks colored or patterned. They carried parasols and fans in their hands. On their feet, they wore shoes of light, flexible leather. Soldiers and workmen wore thick-soled sandals.

A woman could not own land or vote. She was responsible for supervising the household.

The Roman Feast

Wealthy Romans sometimes attended banquets called *cenas* where they ate well and were sometimes entertained by musicians and dancers. Banquet food included staple foods such as bread, olives, onions, and wine, as well as foods only the wealthy could afford, including eggs, meat, chicken, seafood, fruits such as figs, and honeyed wine to drink. The most popular flavoring for Roman meals was *liquamen*, a salty sauce made from fermented fish. Banquet guests reclined on three couches while they ate. Often when women were present, men ate sitting up. Dancers sometimes entertained guests while musicians played music.

Patricians dined in the spacious villas that were their homes. A dining room, called a *triclinium*, had fresco-painted walls and colorful tiled floors. Poor Romans lived in overcrowded apartments and often ate meals they purchased in shops. They rarely ate meat.

Sculpture, Painting, and Mosaics

The Etruscans were expert sculptors and many of their clay and bronze sculptures of gods and people survive today. Roman sculpture borrowed its style from the Etruscans and the Greeks who the Romans admired. Roman statues were elegant and muscular, like Greek statues. During the **republic**, the Roman patricians decorated the floors of their homes with mosaics. Mosaics are tiny pieces of glass, marble, or gem, set in colorful designs in cement. Public baths were also decorated with mosaics and paintings. Walls of temples and homes of the wealthy had colorful frescoes on walls. Frescoes are paintings applied directly onto wet plaster. Scenes depicted mythical animals or gods, or portraits of the owner of the home and his family. Some of these artworks have lasted for centuries.

Metalwork and Pottery

Roman artisans used a pottery wheel to coil long, thin strips of clay to form bowls and jugs. The coiled pottery was made smooth before being baked, or fired, in an oven called a kiln. Romans used pottery for serving dishes such as plates and bowls. During the Roman empire, there were several pottery factories in Italy, France, and Spain where the clay was pushed into plaster molds that formed dishes with decorative designs. The red clay dishes were sold all over the empire.

Philosophy and Writing

Romans adopted ways of learning, called philosophies, from Greece and other empires they conquered or traded with. Roman men studied different philosophies in schools. Sometimes Rome's emperors thought the philosophies were dangerous because they made people question the emperor's power. The works of many famous Roman authors and poets survived and are still studied today. Seneca was a writer and philosopher who wrote about maintaining order and the rule of wise people. His views got him banished from the senate. Virgil wrote a massive poem called the *Aeneid*, which was a history of the first settlers of Rome. Ovid wrote books about the gods, and Horace wrote long poems called satires which made fun of Roman society.

Reporting From a Volcano

In 79 A.D., a volcano on Mount Vesuvius in Italy erupted with such force that it destroyed Pompeii, a coastal town south of Rome. Roman writer and historian Pliny the Elder died while leading a rescue party to Pompeii. Accounts of his death were written in the record of the loss of Pompeii. Debris and ash totally buried the town, including its forums, temples, baths, theaters, and homes. The ash protected the ruins for years. Archaeologists began excavating Pompeii in 1748.

A mosaic found at the entrance to a home in Pompeii, reads "cave canem," or "beware of dog."

Ancient Japan

Most people in ancient Japan lived in small farming communities on land ruled by clans or powerful landowners. Working families shared plots of land and worked together to plant and harvest crops. Many Japanese art forms came from China between 650 A.D. and 1000 A.D. The Japanese adapted these forms over hundreds of years into styles that reflect the Japanese interest in nature and drama.

300 B.C.–1582 A.D.

Farming Rice

Rice farming was difficult and required many people to work together in the fields. The land was divided into separate regions, each ruled by a group, or clan, of powerful warriors called an *uji*. By 57 A.D., more than 100 *uji* controlled the land that made up Japan. Most people did not belong to an *uji*. Instead, they belonged to families of workers who lived on the land controlled by an *uji*. The working families were organized by the type of work they did into groups called *be*. The members of a *be* had to work hard to produce goods for their *uji*. This earned them the right to live on the land. Each *uji* had several *be*, including a farming, pottery, weaving, and fishing *be*.

Women in Japan

Women enjoyed a high status, or rank, in society during the Yayoi and Yamato periods. They were often rulers of clans or fortune tellers called shamans. Women's status changed when the religion of Buddhism and the teachings of Confucius came to Japan from China around 550 A.D. Both traditions taught that women were less important than men. Women were respected only if they were obedient wives and good mothers. As Buddhism and **Confucianism** became more important, women lost many of their rights. They could no longer own property or attend school. From 770 A.D. to 1629 A.D., there were no women rulers in Japan.

Early Japanese noblewomen wore flowing gowns made of silk.

Outside Influence

People in ancient Japan traded with people from ancient Persia, India, China, and Korea. As trade between the nations grew, the Japanese began to borrow some of the traditions of these other cultures. The Japanese adopted Chinese styles of writing, artwork, and government until 894 A.D. After that, the people of ancient Japan changed the Chinese customs to fit with their own ideas and way of life. Many of the cultural traditions of ancient Japan continue to be practiced today. Traditional Japanese entertainment, sports, and martial arts remain important in modern-day Japan. Other aspects of Japanese culture have become popular in many parts of the world.

The Tea Ceremony

Chanoyu, the tea ceremony, was brought to Japan by Buddhist monks from China around 800 A.D. *Chanoyu* was seen as a way to make daily life more beautiful, and eventually became a major part of Japanese culture. The tea ceremony was often included in religious ceremonies. Tea houses were built on stilts and surrounded by beautiful gardens.

Origami

Origami is the art of folding paper. It has been practiced in Japan since 500 A.D. Paper was folded into shapes that had symbolic meaning and were used in **Shinto** ceremonies. The paper was imported from China and was expensive, so only the wealthy did *origami* at first. Once the Japanese learned to make paper, it was used to sculpt useful objects, such as boxes and wallets.

Flower Arranging

Ikebana means the "way of the flower." Buddhist monks in China studied ways of arranging flowers to make beautiful arrangements that helped them **meditate**. The monks brought their flower arranging methods to Japan. *Ikebana* was usually practiced as a pleasant way of passing the time by the upper classes of ancient Japan.

Making *Washi*

Buddhist monks brought papermaking technology to Japan from China around 610 A.D. The Japanese adapted the technique to make their own type of paper, called *washi*. First, stalks of the gampi shrub were boiled in water. Then, the inner bark was beaten into a pulp and poured into tubs full of water and vegetable gum, which made the pulp stick together. The pulp was spread onto screens and dried in the sun to make sheets of paper.

Geisha

In ancient Japan, *geisha* were women who performed music and dance in tea houses and inns. They first appeared during the Heian period (794 A.D.–1192 A.D.). It took many years to become a *geisha*. Girls were educated in Japanese arts such as dancing, music, the tea ceremony, *ikebana*, poetry, and conversation. A *geisha* had to give up her career if she wanted to marry.

Noh Theater

Noh theater developed in Japan around 1350. The plays told stories about *kami*, love, and battles between heroes and evil spirits. The actors wore painted wooden masks instead of makeup. Only men were allowed to perform in noh plays. The actors recited poetry accompanied by music made with drums and flutes.

Ancient sumo competition

A yamato-e *painting depicts a scene from a famous novel called* The Tale of Genji.

Yamato-e Painting

Around 800 A.D., the Japanese developed a style of painting known as *yamato-e*. These were detailed landscapes showing beautiful areas of Japan. *Yamato-e* painting was used to decorate sliding screens that separated rooms in the homes of nobles. They also illustrated stories in books.

Ancient Fighting Techniques

Jujitsu is a style of fighting that developed in Japan over a 2,500-year period. By the 1600s A.D. it was a key part of **samurai** training. Using knowledge of the body's weak spots, a samurai used throws and kicks to take down his opponent. Jujitsu developed into judo in the 1800s, and is practiced all over the world today. Kendo was inspired by samurai sword fighting, but a bamboo stick is used to defend an attack rather than a samurai sword. Karate is the Japanese art of self-defense, and has become very popular in North America.

Sumo Wrestling

The first history of Japan, the *Kojiki*, tells of how two men battled with each other for the ownership of Japan over 2,500 years ago. They fought each other using a style of fighting called sumo wrestling. In sumo matches, opponents grapple with each other in a ring. The first wrestler who is pushed out of the ring loses. Sumo wrestlers weighed up to 400 pounds (180 kg) and were extremely strong. Today, sumo wrestling is Japan's national sport and the best wrestlers are rich and famous. They are treated as heroes.

Ancient Celts

800 B.C.– 43 A.D.

Most Celtic clans lived together in small farming communities. Every house was shared by three generations of a family, including children, their parents, their unmarried aunts and uncles, and their grandparents. The Celts were fond of decoration and made gold, silver, and bronze ornaments for themselves and their horses. They were also known throughout the ancient world for their music, stories, and intricate artwork.

The Homestead

Most Celtic families lived in a farming homestead surrounded by an earth wall or a fence of sharpened logs for defense, called a palisade. The homestead consisted of a main house, a dairy, a smithy, a granary, and sheds for the animals. Across Europe, rectangular houses were common, and some houses in Britain and Ireland were round. Walls were made from stone, planks of wood, or from a wooden frame covered with plaster made of mud and straw. Celtic houses had a single room inside. A fire pit made of flat stones was situated in the center of the room, and a hole in the thatched roof allowed the smoke to escape. Inside the home, the family sat and slept on blankets made of animal skins or woven wool.

The Celts' most common meal was porridge made from oats. They also ate stews made with meat and vegetables, such as turnips and beans, accompanied by small loaves of bread. Bread was made from barley, rye, or wheat flour. The most popular meats were boar, pork, beef, deer, and bear. To wash the food down, Celts drank beer that was brewed by soaking grains, such as wheat or barley, in water. When the grains started to sprout, they were drained of the water and roasted over a fire. Then, they were boiled in water and yeast was added. The brew was left for several weeks while the yeast acted on it. It was then strained to remove the grains. Mead, another common drink, was made in the same way, but honey was added to the water to make it sweeter-tasting than beer.

Celtic Dress

Celtic women wore floor-length dresses made of woven cloth, and wealthy women wore linen and silk dresses. Belts were made of leather or bronze chains. Men wore shirts and knee-length tunics made of linen cloth. Wool was woven into cloth to make warm trousers for the men, long skirts for the women, and cloaks that were fastened with decorative brooches. Both men and women wore leather shoes or sandals.

Celtic women styled their hair with combs made from bone. Hair was worn straight, curled, or in braids, and was decorated with combs and ornaments. Women used oils and sweet herbs as perfume. Celtic men braided or spiked their hair, and often bleached it with **lime** water. Archaeologists have found many mirrors and razors, which they believe were used by nobles.

Celts in Britain and Ireland built large, circular houses similar to these reconstructions. Each house was almost 50 feet (15 meters) in diameter.

Children

From an early age, children were expected to help their parents in the home. Girls were taught how to spin wool and weave cloth, make butter and cheese, cook, and make simple pottery. Boys helped in the fields with the animals, and other farm work. Boys, and girls, if they wished, were taught how to fight with a sword and spear.

Skilled Artisans

Artisans were people who mastered a craft. Blacksmiths, engravers, and glassmakers were paid to make jewelry, weapons, and tools. Learning a skill was a common way for farmers to become wealthier. The children of artisans usually trained to do the same job as their parents. The Celts did not waste any part of an animal that they killed. They made hundreds of different items from animal bones, such as needles, shovels, tool handles, and musical instruments, such as flutes. Leather goods, such as shoes and belts, were made from animal skins, and drinking vessels were made from animal horns.

Celtic designs were some of the most unique and beautiful in the ancient world. Early Celtic art had repeating patterns of triangles, lines, and rectangles, or maze-like patterns running along an item. By 400 B.C., decoration had become more detailed and complex. Fine spirals, leaf shapes, and images of birds, animals, and trees were engraved on metal and wood. Faces of people and animals were often hidden in the patterns and could only be seen when looking at the artwork very closely.

The Celts invented enameling as a form of decoration for jewelry, weapons, and bowls. Melted colored glass was poured onto bronze, silver, or iron objects, which cooled into a hard shiny pattern, like the design on this bowl.

Celtic Women

Some Celtic women were rulers, and many others were druids, bards, or artisans. Women owned property, chose their husbands, and could divorce and remarry if they wished. Some women trained as warriors, although most looked after the children, cooked food, wove cloth, and made pottery for the home.

Myths and Legends

Musicians and poets, known as bards, were highly respected, as their job was to learn the Celtic histories, stories, and legends and recite them as songs or poetry in each community. Bards also carried news between clans. The Celts told stories of heroes and adventure. The stories were written down long after the Celtic culture declined, but they reveal the types of stories druids and bards told 2,000 years ago. One of the most famous stories is that of the Celtic hero, Cú Chulainn, from Ireland. In it, the queen of Ireland sends her men to capture a bull from Cú Chulainn's clan. Cú Chulainn single-handedly defends his people and protects the bull from the queen's men.

Music

The Celts played music in their homes for entertainment in the evenings. Most people made flutes and whistles from bone or wood. Bards told their stories or poems accompanied by drum beats or simple music played on a flute or a stringed harp. Chieftains owned highly decorated wooden and bronze horns that they used to call warriors to battle, to signal during hunts, and to play at feasts. Many horns were decorated with carvings of animals, such as wolves.

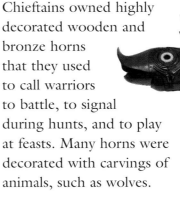

The carnyx, above, was a wind instrument created and played by the Celts.

29

Ancient Vikings

787 A.D.–1100 A.D.

Most Vikings lived on small farms in buildings called longhouses. Families of grandparents, parents, and children lived together in the same house, and everyone in the family worked on the farm. Wealthy families owned slaves to help with hard labor such as removing stones from the farmland. The Vikings filled the cold days of winter and early spring with many feasts and festivals. Gatherings included music, singing, and playing games. Much time was also spent decorating many everyday items with intricate engravings or jewels.

Farming and Fishing

Viking farms had a shed for storing food and larger farms also had a blacksmith's house and a slave hut. Farmers grew vegetables, such as onions, cabbages, and turnips, and grains such as barley, wheat, and flax. They also kept pigs, cows, sheep, and geese on their farms. Horses were used for transportation, and to pull carts and plow fields. From the oceans surrounding their homelands, the Vikings caught fish to eat. They also sailed further out into the Atlantic Ocean to fish for cod, haddock, and mackerel, and to hunt seals, whales, and walruses.

Longhouses

Longhouses were made of blocks of sod, stone, and wood, if it was available. The roofs were thatched with straw, reeds, or heather. They were about ten feet (three meters) wide and 100 feet (30 meters) long, and usually consisted of one room with a central fire pit. Longhouses did not have windows, but a smoke hole in the roof let in light and fresh air.

Viking homes had little furniture. People sat on wooden benches packed with soil that lined the inside walls of the house. The benches were also used as beds and were covered with fur in wealthy households.

Longhouse

Meals and Clothing

Vikings usually ate simple meals twice a day. Breakfast was often bread made of wheat, oats, or rye served with leftover meat. Dinner was either meat roasted on a spit, fish, or a stew of vegetables and meat, such as pork, beef, and mutton.

Most Viking clothing was made from wool. Men wore woolen trousers held up by a strap around the waist or long straps tied around the legs. They also wore woolen undershirts and long-sleeved tunics. Women wore long woolen dresses which they protected with aprons or overdresses. Woolen or fur cloaks kept Vikings warm in cold weather.

Viking clothes were made of wool or linen cloth, which was brightly colored using vegetable dyes. Their clothing was often embroidered, or decorated with colorful thread.

Viking Women

Viking girls were often married between the ages of twelve and fifteen to men chosen by their fathers. As wives, the girls spent their days spinning and weaving cloth from wool, brewing beer and mead, and cooking. Wives also had to look after their farms when their husbands were away. A Viking woman was allowed to divorce her husband if he mistreated or insulted her. She could not inherit property from her parents unless she had no brothers to whom it could go instead.

A Child's Life

Viking children began working when they were around five years old. Girls helped their mothers with weaving, cooking, and brewing beer and mead. The strongest girls were sometimes taught how to use weapons, such as knives, swords, and spears. Boys accompanied their parents as they worked on the farm to learn how to care for crops and animals. They were also taught how to fight with weapons, to navigate, and to build and repair ships. Some boys were sent to work as apprentices to blacksmiths or other artisans.

Musical Entertainment

The Vikings sang and played music at home, as well as at festivals, feasts, and funerals. Panpipes and hornpipes were made from cow horns or sheep bones. The Vikings also played lyres, which were similar to guitars, and rebecs, which were like violins. The strangest-looking musical instrument was the *lur*. This was a long, cone-shaped wooden wind instrument that sounded like a deep trumpet.

Activities

The Vikings participated in activities, such as sledding, skiing, and skating. These were also common forms of transportation in winter. Vikings enjoyed indoor activities, such as board games. One of the most popular board games was called *Hnefatafl*, meaning "knight's table." This game was very similar to modern chess, and was played in many countries throughout Europe.

Hnefatafl *game pieces were made of antler, bone, clay, stone, glass, or wood.*

Decoration

Viking art was used to make everyday items look attractive. Dishes, pots, chests, and weapons such as shields were engraved with **runes** or painted with images of mythical beasts, gods, and warriors. A common Viking decoration was the gripping beast, believed to ward off evil. Long, thin creatures with tendrils were carved winding up and around an object.

Many Viking artisans were skilled engravers and jewelers. One of the most common types of jewelry made by Viking blacksmiths was arm or neck rings made of silver. Chieftains often had these rings made for themselves and their wives as a sign of wealth. Other jewelry was made of glass beads that were strung together. Many of the beads had yellow and black stripes, and were known as wasp beads. Metal jewelry was engraved with designs of interwoven curves and lines. Men wore silver pendants of the hammer of Thor, the thunder god. These pendants were thought to protect sailors against drowning and danger.

Wooden Viking shields were painted with colorful designs.

Glossary

aqueduct A channel for carrying fresh water

Buddhism A religion founded by Buddha, an ancient religious leaders from India

city-state An independent city, usually walled for defense, and the surrounding towns and villages that depend upon it for defense

concubine A mistress or secondary wife

Confucianism A system of ethics and philosophy based on the teachings of Chinese scholar Confucius

dowry The property that a woman brings to her husband in marriage

dynasty A series of rulers from the same family

ferment To allow a substance to change over time, usually into a new product, such as alcohol

fertility The ability to produce life

flax A plant used to make cloth, oil, and animal feed

fresco A kind of painting done on fresh moist plaster with colors dissolved in water

geometric Simple designs based on squares, triangles, and circles

guru A great teacher

hieroglyph A picture or symbol used to represent the meaning or sound of words and letters

inherit To receive money or property after someone's death

iron oxide Iron that is combined with oxygen

legume Foods such as peas, beans, and lentils

lime A white chemical, also called calcium oxide, which is used in making mortar and cement

meditate The act of thinking quietly

mosaic A decoration on a surface made by setting small colored pieces of glass or stone into another material to make patterns

nobles People who have a high position in society

nomadic Moving from place to place

pastoral Relating to the country or country life

philosophy A set of beliefs about life and the world

reliefs Stone carvings in which figures are raised from the background

republic A state or system of government where power rests with citizens who vote for their leaders

rune Characters of the Viking alphabet

sacred Having special religious meaning

sacrifice An offering to a god or a goddess

samurai A class of warrior in ancient Japan

scribe A person who makes a living by copying or recording text

Shinto The first religion practiced in Japan, which combined a love of nature with the worship of ancestor spirits

smelt The process of removing a metal from an ore, usually by melting

thatched Straw or grass woven to make a roof

tunic A long, loose piece of clothing worn by men and women

utensil A tool, such as s fork, used to pick up food

whitewashed Whitened with a mix of water and lime

yeast A substance made up of fungi that grow quickly

Index

Websites

www.bbc.co.uk/history/ancient/
Amazing images highlight in-depth looks into ancient cultures.

www.historyforkids.org/
This site provides information on the history, food, clothing, technology, stories, and religion of many ancient cultures.

www.pbs.org/wgbh/nova/ancient/
Interactive videos take readers through ancient civilizations.

www.archaeolink.com/amazing_worlds_of_archaeology1.htm
This site provides links to sites with archaeological information.

Further Reading

Ancient Art and Cultures series, Rosen Publishing Group 2010

Life in Ancient Times series, Gareth Stevens Publishing 2010

Ancient Communities series, Powerkids Press 2010

Ancient Civilizations and Their Myths and Legends series, Rosen Central 2009

Biography from Ancient Civilizations: Legends, Folklore, and Stories of Ancient Worlds series, Mitchell Lane Publishers 2009